WALKING
Blind

Damilola Gbadamosi

Walking Blind

To everyone and anyone that is ready and willing to gain his or her sight and willing to walk in the light

ACKNOWLEDGMENTS

I will be ungrateful not to acknowledge my Heavenly Father for His grace and mercies towards me. Thank you, Lord Jesus, for your unending love towards me. Thank you, Holy Spirit, for your guidance and inspiration.

A big thank you goes to my Mother, Taiwo Gbadamosi, for always being supportive. You have always been there and I pray God grants you long life to enjoy the fruit of your labor.

To my mentor and father, Oreofe Williams, thank you so much for your words of wisdom and encouragement.

Pastor Sam Elijah, your words of encouragement and prayers has helped shape me into a better person. Thank you so much sir.

Sister Toyin Jtutu, my ever loving and awesome sister. Thank you for being you, you are the best sister anyone could ever ask for.

Mummy Ziona Qing, I appreciate you for always interceding for me in prayers, advising me and motivating me to be a better person.

Ayo Emannuel Ojo, my ever-supportive brother, you are the best brother anyone could ever ask for. You always go out of your way for me and God bless you for that.

Olatide Egbinola, my prayer and worship partner and sister, I love you to the moon and back. And to everyone who has impacted me one way or the other and everyone reading this book. God bless you!

TABLE OF CONTENTS

BLINDNESS

A Christian that is lukewarm or blind is a believer that has allowed the ways of the world to dominate or determine his movements. Believing in the things that the world had to offered and selling his right as an exchanged for darkness

WHAT IS BLINDNESS?

B lindness is the lack of vision. It can also be described as a loss of vision. Blindness is the inability to see correctly or the inability to see beyond the walls. Often times, scriptures employ the use of imagery of blindness in explaining spiritual conditions, or the spiritual state of individuals who are not where they are supposed to be and are ignorant about it or those that lack the revelation of the intents and mind of the creator for the things that are created.

It must be understood that the things of God cannot be seen or perceived by the physical eyes or by an historical journey of scientific permutations and combinations but by the revelation of God to an individual. Once an individual cannot see the things of God from the non-physical realm, such an individual is said to be blind. *(Matt 11:25-27; 1 Cor. 1:21; 2 Peter 1:19-21). It is the Lord who "gives sight to the blind" (Psalm 146:8; Isa 42:16).*

In the Old Testament, Isaiah was a prophet of God that dwelt on the topic of blindness as the basis for people to move into perfect light. Beholding and seeing as they should never mixing things together but basking in the revelation of God and having a glimpse into God's will and purpose for His children. The blindness of the Israelites was a rebellious act in Isaiah's sight, announcing it to their faces and admonishing them on the proper way to go *(43:8; 56:10; 59:10).* Zephaniah reveals that this condition is divinely imposed upon the hardhearted *(1:17).* Due to the continuous disobedience of the people of Israel, God ordained appropriately that the messiah was going to come to give light, with his ministry being marked by light. *(Isaiah 42:7 Isaiah 42:16 Isaiah 42:18).*

At the beginning of Christ ministry, Jesus spelt out to the people of Israel of his intentions to fulfill the prophecies as spoken from the mouth of Prophet Isaiah, *"recovering the sight of the blind and making men see what they should by breaking them out the bondage of darkness" (Luke 4:18).*

If the life of Jesus is scrutinized, many of his comments, outburst or outcries were directed at the Pharisees mainly for their lack of vision, sight and their inability to dwell in light, which in essence is Christ the redeemer Himself. The Pharisees feigned themselves as righteous haven believed and lived life according to Jewish laws and commandment obeying every part of the law with a mindset of proving to the world that they are saints, a condition which Jesus describe as a blind state. Jesus ascription of the Pharisees as the *"blind guides of the blind" (Matt 15:14; 23:16-26; John 9:39-41)* came as a form of the description of the state they were, due to their rigidness to continue in a place of non-understanding. He then announces that He will impose judgment on these self-righteous legalists, *"so that the blind will see and those who see will become blind" (John 9:39).*

After Jesus died, rose, and went into the heavens, the church had people that were also *"corpse among the living"* as Paul described them.

In their case the god of this world had blinded the minds of the unbelievers, to keep them from seeing the light of the gospel of the glory of Christ, who is the image of God *2 Corinthians 4:4.*

Paul was quick to note that blindness was a state for the pagans. Blindness is the state of a Gentile, the normal life for an unbeliever

People that don't believe him or reject him are lost *(John 6:68-69)*. Because of this, they are spiritually blind and they are considered as perishable goods in the hands of the master. *(2 Corinthians 4:3-4; Revelation 3:17)*.

They have decided not to accept his teachings, ways, knowledge and his Lordship over their lives. They are usually described as those who *"do not accept the things of the Spirit of God, for they are folly to him, and he is not able to understand them because they are spiritually discerned" (1 Corinthians 2:14)*.

Therefore, a believer is supposed to be one full of light, alienated from the world of darkness.

Blindness is a disease that is caused by the god of this age, the intent of the god of the age is to make people invisible to the things of God and make the things of God far from them so that they will not reap the benefits of what Christ has come to do for them.

If you note in that verse, to keep them from seeing the light of the gospel of the glory of Christ, who is the image of God.

The purpose of the devil in dominating a believers life with darkness is to keep a believer blind and their minds away from the glory of the Gospel, which is the revelation of Christ *(Roman 1:16-17)*.

So, when a man is blinded, he can't see the treasure of that glory, all he sees is another way of walking which is not Christ-like

New Testament believers must also understand that they can be blind due to their carefree attitudes towards the things of God.

Apostle Peter charges Christians in *2 Peter 1:7-10* to be careful, ensuring activeness and open sight

In the book of revelation, John described the Laodician church as blind and lukewarm. A Christian that is lukewarm or blind is a believer that has allowed the ways of the world to dominate or determine his movements. Believing in the things that the world had to offer and selling his right as an exchange for darkness.

Spiritual blindness is also the ability not to see Christ. We must understand that the Holy Spirit has not only come as our helper but to make an unveiling of the Christ. *"When the Spirit of truth comes, he will guide you into all the truth, for he will not speak on his own authority, but whatever he hears he will speak, and he will declare to you the things that are to come". (John 16:13)*

When a believer does not allow the works of the Holy Spirit in the aspect of the unveiling of Christ to him; such a believer can be said to be blind' why because that believer is unable to comprehend spiritual truths cannot understand the word of God as he should. Causing a myopic view of the word of God in head knowledge but never getting the revelation of what Christ wants to really communicate.

When an individual is spiritually blind, he cannot see Christ and not to see Christ is not to see God *(Colossians 1:15-16; 2 Corinthians 4:6)*. Spiritual blindness is usually a dangerous condition of people who do not know God, believe in God, Jesus Christ, and His Word *(Romans 2:8; 2 Thessalonians 2:12)*.

Therefore, it can be said that a blind believer is such who cannot comprehend the truth of God's word. Limiting Christ's mystery to the physical communications (letters). *"In their case the god of this world has blinded the minds of the unbelievers, to keep them from seeing the light of the gospel of the glory of Christ, who is the image of God".* *2 Corinthians 4:4*

According to this scripture, blindness is the inability to see the light of the gospel. Someone asks, what is the gospel? The Gospel is the good news which is Christ was sent to die for the sin of the world and He resurrected on the third day. *"For God so loved the world, that he gave his only Son, that whoever believes in him should not perish but have eternal life".* *John 3: 16*

In other words, Blindness is the inability to see the light of the good news.

Paul ascribed spiritual blindfolding to the works of Satan. Satan works are evil, a degeneration from the truth of God. The objectives of Satan in any man's life is to have his works in his flesh, bringing to naught every provision of God to him. *"So that we would not be outwitted by Satan; for we are not ignorant of his designs"* *2 Corinthians 2:11*

Satan's goal is to devour the weak who fall prey to temptation, fear, loneliness, worry, depression, and persecution. Without the power of God in a man's life. Satan can devour anything, controlling the man as he wills and subjecting him to his desires and will for the world.

What is light?

Again, Jesus spoke to them, saying, *"I am the light of the world. Whoever follows me will not walk in darkness, but will have the light of life." John 8:12*

The term **"light"** has been fully described by this scripture which emphasizes on the fact that Jesus is the light. To be able to see the light, **"Jesus",** one needs to be in right standing with God.

Jesus answered him, *"Truly, truly, I say to you, unless one is born again he cannot see the kingdom of God." John 3:3*

Being born again in this scripture does not mean going back to your mother's womb and be conceived again, rather, it means accepting Jesus Christ as your personal Lord and Savior. In other words, if you cannot see the light, you cannot see the Kingdom of God.

What is Darkness?

They are darkened in their understanding, alienated from the life of God because of the ignorance that is in them, due to their hardened heart. Ephesians 4:18

Darkness, according to this scripture is caused by ignorance and hardness of heart. Of course, when one refuses to see and follow the light of God which is Christ Jesus, the person is in total darkness

PRAYER POINT: *Lord Jesus, please open my eyes that I may see the light. Amen.*

BLIND LEADER

Let them alone; they are blind guides. And if the blind lead the blind, both will fall into a pit. Matthew 15:14

BLIND LEADER

L*et them alone; they are blind guides. And if the blind lead the blind, both will fall into a pit.*
Matthew 15:14

Having blind followers is bad enough; however, having a blind leader with blind followers is simply horrible. If a group of blind followers are with a leader who sees the light, he might be able to direct them in the way of the light. The scripture explains it perfectly, when the blind leads the blind, they will both fall into a pit.

Many scriptures have foretold the future of Israel, describing their future blindness because of the things they indulged in. the major strength of those prophecies were their intents, showing the state of the leadership of the nation as blind

Jeremiah in his writings spoke of a time Israel would be led by strange prophets, causing them to err from the promises, laws and commandments of God. *"For the house of Israel and the house of Judah have been utterly treacherous to me, declares the Lord. They have spoken falsely of the Lord and have said, He will do nothing; no disaster will come upon us, nor shall we see sword or famine. The prophets will become wind; the word is not in them. Thus, shall it be done to them!" Jeremiah 5:11-13*

What Jeremiah was trying to point out is a generation of scrupulous prophets that will speak the word of God in disguise with a lying-tongue, blaspheming the word of God.

The reason for the destruction of Israel according to the text is the bad leaders that led them. When an individual or a nation, people, country, or an association is led by people who are in darkness, they will always end up in destruction.

The mistakes of the leaders can be reflective on the followers because they are often misguided. This often than not, always leads to a destructive path unto an unending pain and suffering.

Christian leaders or religious leaders are always in a position to lead people alright or mislead them. The direction of one's path is usually based on the sight of the leader.

A leader without sight is usually in the process of misleading his flock. Jesus described the Pharisees as blind leading to blind. *Let them alone; they are blind guides. And if the blind lead the blind, both will fall into a pit. Matthew 15:14*

As discussed in the previous chapter, a blind Christian is one that lacks the understanding of the truth of God's word. A blind Christian leader is one that lacks the understanding of God's word.

A group of blind men decided to go out by themselves when their guide didn't show up on time. They chose a leader amongst themselves and formed a line holding the person in front of them by the shoulder. Of course, this is a route they take on a daily basis so they believed they already knew the way. Without knowing there was a pothole a few steps away from the gate they started their journey. On getting to the pothole, the leader tripped and fell. Immediately, all the followers also found themselves on the floor. There was no one to call upon and they didn't know which direction led back home until the initial guide came around and saw them by the entrance.

A blind leader is usually characterized by a lot of things ranging from holding onto the traditions of men, as in the case of the Pharisees in Matt 15.

Also, they are also characterized by these:

- Making description where God has not (Matthew 23)

- Disobedience to the command of God. (Matthew 23: 23-24)

- Focus on the outer man, that is the things that will perish with the flesh (Matthew 23:25-28)

- They do their works and acts to be seen of men - Matthew 23:5

- They love attention and always want special treatment by others - Matthew 23:6-7

- They pride in their religious titles, exhorting Men to worship their titles - Matthew 23:8-10

- They fail to explain scriptures by revelation and to show the way to the kingdom of God- Matthew 23:13

- They use their titles to enrich their pockets and impress others - Matthew 23:14

A Christian can be saved from the prey of these blind leaders by paying attention to the sayings of the Lord from His word and His spirit. When an individual has a relationship with the Holy Spirit, such individual will always understand the truth, so that he can call to judgment everything that is false and not founded on God's word. *The end of blind leaders will always be destruction they shall be utterly uprooted from the earth and their names erased from the hearts of men. Lord. Then the disciples came and said to him, do you know that the Pharisees were offended when they heard this saying?" He answered, "Every plant that my heavenly Father has not planted will be rooted up. Matthew 15:12-13*

For many of their followers, because of the blind nature of their movements, they shall all fall into the pit with their leader, darkened in their minds unto the gospel of the Lord.

Many people think that leaders are the only ones held accountable for misappropriating the scriptures and misguiding acts; the scriptures however, tells us that even the follower shall be partakers in the suffering. The reason being every believer has been given the earnest of the spirit to work with, revealing unto them the mystery of Christ. *In him you also, when you heard the word of truth, the gospel of your salvation, and believed in him, were sealed with the promised Holy Spirit, 14: who is the guarantee of our inheritance until we acquire possession of it, to the praise of his glory. Ephesians 1:13-14*

Once a Christian is able to communicate with the spirit, he will be granted the spirit of wisdom and revelation to show him God's knowledge and his inheritance in God. But once a believer or a person decides not to do this and hides under the umbrella of a blind leader, he will also be destroyed with the leader. *"To lead people, walk beside them ... As for the best leaders, the people do not notice their existence. The next best, the people honor and praise. The next, the people fear; and the next, the people hate ... When the best leader's work is done, the people say, 'We did it ourselves!'"*— *Lao-tsu*

Leadership is the ability to establish standards and manage a creative climate where people are self-motivated toward the mastery of long term constructive goals, in a participatory environment of mutual respect.

Ask yourself these simple questions and apply this to your day to day life;

Who is your leader?

Who is your mentor?

Who is your role model?

Who are the people that influence you?

Who is the person you run to for advice?

Who is your pastor?

Who are these people? Have you taken your time to study them? How do they react when they are happy, sad, and angry? How is their family? What impacts do they make in the society? Do they adhere to their preaching's, sermons, or even motivations? Be aware, do not walk blindly.

PRAYER POINT: *Holy Spirit, please direct me to the right Leader. Separate me from every bad leader in Jesus name. Amen.*

FELLOWSHIP IN DARKNESS

There is no correlation between light and darkness.

If we say we have fellowship with him while we walk in darkness, we lie and do not practice the truth. 1 John 1:6

FELLOWSHIP IN DARKNESS

What does it mean to fellowship in darkness? People love deceiving themselves when the scripture clearly states in *Revelations 3:16* that you can only be hot or cold. Some still prefer to be lukewarm. Fellowship without LIGHT is fellowship in darkness. *How can you say you acknowledge Christ yet, you do things that are not Christ-Like?* The church of God has become a social gathering filled with so many atrocities and false doctrines. Anything contrary to the scripture should not be practiced, period.

There is no correlation between light and darkness. Fellowship with darkness is equal to deceiving yourself. Some sororities claim to be Christian based yet doctrines practiced are giving reference to the ways of the world, blindfolding Christians by the luxury that is shared in the house of God. Take no part in the unfruitful works of darkness, but instead expose them. Ephesians 5: 11

A difficult part of the Christian journey is breaking away from old habits or works of the enemy. Most times, it is usually difficult for the renewed mind to relate to the people of the world reason being, what Christ does by his gospel in our lives is reconfiguration of our nature to for his own making it hard for us to relate to the world freely.

One of the things that God wants from us is to learn how to break away from all forms of darkness and fellowship with evil The scripture is clear regarding relationship with the world and how a Christian must handle such; *"do not be unequally yoked with unbelievers. For what partnership has righteousness with lawlessness? Or what fellowship has light with darkness? 2Corimthians 6:14*

Fellowship means a communion or in literal terms, a relationship. A relationship is always based on a common ground. That is, I can only have relationship with someone I can agree with *(Amos 3:3)*. When there is a basis of agreement, then we can say that we are in communion or we have fellowship together. *One of the things Christ did for us was to bring us away from the world and the ways of darkness into His marvelous light. "Giving thanks to the Father, who has qualified you to share in the inheritance of the saints in light. He has delivered us from the domain of darkness and transferred us to the kingdom of his beloved Son, in whom we have redemption, the forgiveness of sins. Colossians 1:12-14*

The word *"delivered"* is the word *"rescue"* which means to save, this means that at the point of salvation, you were brought away from the power of darkness and changed or let me say, given a new citizenship in Christ. You were delivered and rescued from darkness, from sin, from shame, and given a new identity through Christ.

Many times, Satan comes in his deceptive nature, bringing to us something that looks like light. But our understanding of God will make it possible for us not to fall prey to his ways, or take on his identity. *Do not be deceived: "Bad company ruins good morals I Corinthians 15:33*

We are being admonished as Christians to understand the ways of God, check our ways always and ensure that we have no fellowship with darkness. Being pure in all our ways is by walking in the Grace that God has provided.

The only way that we can avoid fellowshipping with darkness is to be grounded in God's word, and allowing the domination of His word upon our souls and in our hearts. When this is done, the spirit of God will translate His word to become life to us, making it possible for us to live like we ought to.

When you fellowship with darkness, there is an open door for Satan and its cohorts to have their desires met in your life. Feeding you with unholy details and making you an entity of dark wills and evil mindsets. This has a way of bringing you out of fellowship with God, ensuring non-adherence to His words and desires. *For all that is in the world the desires of the flesh and the desires of the eyes and pride of life is not from the Father but is from the world. 1 John 2: 16*

Fellowship with darkness is usually a strong temptation that most of the times can be difficult to say no to, that is why as a Christian; always ensure you stay in God's shadow where you can be kept safe and free from every form of falling.

PRAYER POINT: *I denounce every fellowship in darkness I have associated myself with in Jesus name. Holy Spirit, please help me to discern every spirit that comes my way in Jesus name. Amen*

EXCESS SLEEP

And a great windstorm arose, and the waves were breaking into the boat, so that the boat was already filling. But he was in the stern, asleep on the cushion. And they woke him and said to him, "Teacher, do you not care that we are perishing? Mark 4:37

EXCESS SLEEP

The word "sleep" is usually translated as the state of the body in an unconscious experience. Also, sleeping can sometimes mean to rest. . But sleeping can also be a form of bad habit especially when an individual indulges in it too much. Sleep is scientifically good as Jesus also slept. *And a great windstorm arose, and the waves were breaking into the boat, so that the boat was already filling. But he was in the stern, asleep on the cushion. And they woke him and said to him, "Teacher, do you not care that we are perishing? (Mark 4:37)*

As much as sleep is a good thing, sleep is also used in the scriptures to describe a lazy Christian Sleep connotes laziness in a Chritian's relationship with God and the lack of diligence in service to God. "Awake, you who are sleeping, and arise from the dead, and Christ shall shine on you" (Ephesians. 5:14).

Sleep can also mean the act of been unprepared, suggesting a non-defensive mood of Christians especially in these last days.

God tells us to wake up. We all need physical sleep, so there is nothing wrong with sleeping at the proper time. But when it is time to wake up, it can be disastrous not to do so.

Though it is always an optional thing, sleeping most of time (spiritual sleep) comes unconsciously. A believer might be unconsciously sleeping and he doesn't know. Excess sleep is a detriment to our spiritual life as it determines how whether or not God is in you.

Every Christian is on a spiritual journey that encompasses a lot fighting and wars. This fighting isn't with any physical element or entity. It is purely a spiritual fight. *For we do not wrestle against flesh and blood, but against the rulers, against the authorities, against the cosmic powers over this present darkness, against the spiritual forces of evil in the heavenly places. 13 Therefore take up the whole armor of God that you may be able to withstand in the evil day, and having done all, to stand firm. Ephesians 6:12*

And because of these powers that we war with, it is essential that we are always awake, guided with every sense of knowledge to be able to stand in these last days. *"A little sleep, a little slumber, A little folding of the hands to rest; So, your poverty will come like a prowler, And you want like an armed man" (Proverbs 24:33-34).*

The best way Satan can take advantage of a believer is to ensure he is spiritually asleep. This is one of the ways he can make such a believer lose his or her glorious riches of Christ Jesus and that is why we must always be awake to the truth of God's word. Being awake doesn't mean you won't take a physical naps or sleep at night; it simply means having a sense of security and safety at all times whether awake or asleep.

To be spiritually awake at all times, a believer must dwell in the word of God, have a praying lifestyle, listen to the spirit, and take caution on every form of excessive sleep. To destroy the plan of the enemy concerning the church, we've being appointed as watchmen by God and we must continue to deny ourselves of sleep to secure the church of Christ and His flocks. *So you, son of man, I have made a watchman for the house of Israel. Whenever you hear a word from my mouth, you shall give them warning from me. Ezekiel 33:7*

The process of watching is to be awake and that's the reasons why we are encouraged in the scriptures to always watch and pray because the adversary (the devil), watches daily for whom to devour (consume). It is therefore in our watching through prayers, the word of God, and declarations of the power of God upon situations and our environment that we are able to destroy the devices of the enemy, bringing to naught his powers and every of his thoughts. *"Awake to righteousness, and do not sin; for some do not have the knowledge of God. I speak this to your shame" (1 Corinthians 15:34).*

One of the clarion calls of God to believers in these last days is to stay awake and be alert. Because of the religious minds of Christian leaders, we have passed a corruptible seed into the body devoid of the sanctification of God.

But Christ has beckoned on us; every believer must come to righteous learning, living and acts. It must not be found among us unholy communications, attitudes and acts because that is what Grace has called us unto.

We have been called to a sacred house, a consecrated assembly and a separated way, it is expected of us to ensure our standing by being awake at all times; prepared for battle and wars that are unseen, so that we can always win having an attitude of an overcomer.

PRAYER POINT: *Lord please help me to stay alert in your strength so that I am always prepared against the evil days. Amen.*

IGNORANCE

They are darkened in their understanding, alienated from the life of God because of the ignorance that is in them, due to their hardness of heart.

Ephesians 4:18

IGNORANCE

The Scripture explains how people are in darkness due to ignorance and stubbornness. Ignorance they say is a disease. Some people are ignorant not because they don't know but they choose not to know. They shut their hearts to the truth and decide to continue dining and wining in darkness, forgetting that the devil is deceitful and will entice you with beauty and luxury until one falls into his trap.

Assuming you did not know the details of what you are about to get into before, what happens to getting help and renouncing it after coming into knowledge of it.

Ignorance is not an excuse when it comes to spiritual things. It is understandable that sometimes, we get deeply involved in things we are not supposed to before realizing it; however it is not too late to make amends. Some people claim to be young so they want to enjoy the days of their youths by doing the things of the world and later apologize to God forgetting that God cannot be mocked. Yes, God is just and would forgive everyone who genuinely repents but what is the guarantee that you will be alive tomorrow *"Now this I ... testify in the Lord, that you must no longer walk as the Gentiles do, in the futility of their minds. They are ... alienated from the life of God because of the ignorance that is in them, due to their hardness of heart"* - Ephesians 4:17-19

God's sovereign mercy and grace is prominent in our lives. We are dead in our souls, wallowing in sin, and having no capacity to save ourselves. What the creator has come to do is to save our soul from sin and deliver our soul into the perfect light. Our Lord must bring back our souls from death if we are by faith going to lay hold on the provision of the righteousness of Christ, which only is the guarantee for our purity, giving us a right standing before God.

Paul's call to the children of Israel not to walk as the gentiles do is not to distinguish ethnic groups or speak against the gentiles. But a call to live the kind of life God wants for every believer which is according to a preordained thought and mindset.

Ignorance is a major excuse in many organizations; people believe they can have what they want based on the platter of ignorance. It is always assumed that doing anything without the knowledge of it should be forgiven if such comes with an error and mistakes. People in ancient African culture killed and made sacrifices to unknown gods on the basis of belief and trust in what their God will do through their sacrifices. This may be forgiven as they were never without knowledge, lacking the necessary civilization to direct their environment in the right way.

In the Old Testament, the gentiles were categorized as igno-rant because they lack the knowledge of God. Never knowing what they were doing, believing in gods made with hands, that couldn't speak, talk but following doggedly strict rules and believing that it is right to live the kind of life which is not acceptable in the presence of God.

But the scripture says in the book of Romans. *For his invisible attributes, namely, his eternal power and divine nature have been clearly perceived, ever since the creation of the world, in the things that have been made. So, they are without excuse. Romans 1:20*

That scripture is a basis to explain to all that has ever lived that ignorance though is justified, but also never justified. The things of God usually has been explained by the things that are created, the eternal qualities of God, his eternal deity, his wish, his mind, his purposes, his miracles, his signs and everything about him has been made visible by the things that are created so that nobody will give an excuse.

Therefore, even though the knowledge of God had not gone widely in the past, God still expects that everyone would learn of him, even if it is through the things that he has created.

Ignorance is an act that God frowns at even from the beginning of the ages. *Guard your steps when you go to the house of God. To draw near to listen is better than to offer the sacrifice of fools, for they do not know that they are doing evil. Ecclesiastes 5:1*

Ignorance is below par to the knowledge that has been made available. When knowledge is made available, the non-sensitivity to such knowledge is an ignorant act. The ability to live life without entering the door of knowledge can be defined as ignorance. Many people have violated the laws of God in their ignorance, never coming to that knowledge.

Philosophers have gone near and far, looking for knowledge to prove everything that they believe in, striving to just understand a minuet part of Gods. Scientists have gone wide and far, done researches and tested all things to bring to naught the existence of God, but throughout their search, they have never found that which they are confident of.

Ignorance is a blindfold on the human nature, everybody that is not of God is blinded by another form of life that is corruption. Ignorance is a nature that blinds a man from seeing afar and walking according to His instructions rather than the instruction of things that are seen. A man is ignorant if he doesn't believe in the ways of God; he is alienated from the commonwealth of Zion and being ruled by the spirit of disobedience.

An unbeliever is ignorant of the truth of God, because he cannot discern them. The mystery of the Lord is kept away from him and he cannot see them because they are not physically experienced but spiritually discerned. Every physical effort of an unbeliever to find explanation for the things of God will always come to fruitlessness and unbarring because of his ignorance to know the things of God.

Except a person comes into Christ, he will always be ignorant of the things that are created. We must see this and that is why it is essential that we proclaim the gospel as believers, telling people about the good news of Christ. This will give the unbelievers the accurate knowledge of God for mankind and the things he has done.

Every unbeliever is entitled, destined, called to this knowledge and escape the ignorance that set the world behind in the things of God.

Walking Blind

Ignorant Christians

And he said, "Are you also still without understanding? Matthew 15:16

Or do you presume on the riches of his kindness and forbearance and patience, not knowing that God's kindness is meant to lead you to repentance? Romans 2:4

Notice that in the above scriptures, Jesus and Paul were emphatic in bringing to light the ignorance of the Christian faith. Many Christians even though have accepted God are still alienated from the understanding that God has brought them into light. Many fail in the test of time, trying to explain God by the physical structure of their minds.

In the book of Matthew, Jesus put it to his disciples, *'are you also even dull and ignorant'?* Ignorance as a Christian is the lack of spiritual understanding or the inability to assimilate the knowledge of God.

A good example is a person who professes Christ and serve him in his house, sing songs during services, jump around with hope and always attentive to Pastor's word. When faced with a little issue, he or she withdraws from God's presence because of the lack of faith in Him for sustenance. Shaken and fearful, failing to understand that *'the trials of your faith worketh patience'*. Even though such a believer have lived and enjoyed the things of God, he is ignorant of some of his rights in Christ, his knowledge of God is shallow and he is still a baby, sucking milk and never growing up. Such a believer is not grounded and the deep things of God cannot be entrusted to him.

44

This kind of believer needs to be prayed for and taken to a true church where he can be grounded in the things of God, or for one that is already among the true brethren, he needs to open his mind and give more time to the word of God and prayer. This will give him the opportunity of continually beholding what God has come to do and his promises for his generation. Learning the right ways of truth and fulfilling the things of God and his wish for the present age.

Hardness of the heart

Even though sometimes Ignorance of a believer is justifiable and can still be forgiven. But the results of a hardened heart are usually a strong opposite heart to the truth. Ignorance has a way of coming into the mind of a believer and gives him a stony heart which isn't willing to learn.

The hardness of heart comes by the way of not receiving the truth in meekness. It was stated that if a believer is ignorant, he needs to learn the word of God by being grounded in a true church. But there are some that are still established in a true church and never learning. Not because they are not hearing but because their hearts are hardened to the word of God and they cannot receive his light into their heart. These kinds of people are fools thinking they can always buy away everything by physical words and actions. They are ever wanting to learn but never able to grasp that knowledge because of the state of their hearts.

Hardness is the state of the human mind and heart not to receive, comprehend, understand, and process the things of God. It must be noted that unbelievers that fail to accept Jesus after their message of the gospel is preached is ignorant and has a hardened heart. It must also be said that a believer is also subject to this life because of the ways he can live his life.

The knowledge of God comes as a form of light in his word for many that are ready to receive him.

The parable of Jesus clearly depicts the kind of life an ignorant and a stubborn person will live. A Christian is opened to the things of the Lord in all ways, that is, he can actually get it right by the provision the Lord has made through his words and suffering. The word of God is available for as many individual and daily the Lord sows his word into the air every day for as many that are willing to receive.

In describing the parable of the sower, Jesus depicted seed that fell on the sand, wayside and amidst the thorns as the bad ground. The word of the Lord is good always but when the seed of the word comes into the heart, only the state of the heart can make it grow.

For a Christian without knowledge, because of the non-fertile ground of the heart, such is not able to grow and become who they are supposed to be. And many of these occur because of the hardness of the heart, the stinginess of the human is to receive what God has for it and the stiff attitude of the ignorant man.

So many things can cause the hardening of the heart, environment, the style of growth; life situations can also harden your heart. Opened to us is the events and situations that can get us offended, wounding our hearts in that course by hardening it. Different word from people, anger, disappointments of life, complacency and so many things that surrounds us.

To avoid the hardness of heart, we can pick from the points below so that we can daily wash our hearts, understanding the need to be humble totally to the Lord, ready to learn at every given chance.

Submission to God and his word is the most paramount thing in learning the ways of God. When we are able to submit to the word of God through studying and prayer, we will be able to learn the ways of the Lord making our heart humble in that way.

For this people's heart has grown dull, and with their ears they can barely hear and their eyes they have closed; lest they should see with their eyes and hear with their ears and understand with their heart and turn, and I would heal them Act 28:27

The word of God works upon the soul and makes it soft, so that he is able to learn rightly the things that God will have him learn. The beginning of the softening of heart is to recognize and submit to God's word and authority.

PRAYER POINT: *Holy Spirit, help me to be willing and open to walking in the Light of God. In Jesus name. AMEN.*

WICKEDNESS

And this is the judgment: the light has come into the world, and people loved the darkness rather than the light because their works were evil.

John 3:19

WICKEDNESS

One of the things that are most prevalent in the world is the degeneration of behaviors and attitudes that have encompassed the people, bringing them into a state of unholy doings.

The Hebrew word for wickedness that is used in the scriptures is "rish`ah", which means guilt, a criminal qualification of one that has done something very bad. Wickedness is an abominable act, since the dawn of creation. *Now the men of Sodom were wicked, great sinners against the Lord. Genesis 13:13*

Wickedness has always been something the Lord abhor with an intention to remove it from sight. God has not ordained any believer unto wickedness.

The Greek word for wickedness is "ponēria", meaning iniquity, depravity, malice, etc. wickedness is the ability to do evil willingly without any form of repentance or conscience pricking. Satan wickedness started when he wanted to take over throne in heaven causing a war among the heavenly creatures. *How you are fallen from heaven, O Day Star, son of Dawn! How you are cut down to the ground, you who laid the nations low! You said in your heart, I will ascend to heaven; above the stars of God. I will set my throne on high; I will sit on the mount of assembly in the far reaches of the north; I will ascend above the heights of the clouds: I will make myself like the Most High. But you are brought down to Sheol, to the far reaches of the pit. (Isaiah 14:12-15)*

Because of the act of Satan, God sent him away from heaven into banishment, away from the heavenly riches and glory because of his wicked nature. An act that made him determine that every individual was going to be like him.

As a reason of that, he planned to sow into every man the wicked act of evil, to allow for unholy behaviors from the saints of God, who had been predestined to be good, righteous and holy until the day of the Lord.

The definition of wickedness is firstly not about the act but the heart. Wickedness is a powerful element of a corrupt heart, everything that an unholy heart does is wickedness because it becomes a nature unto him. *Ask, and it will be given to you; seek, and you will find; knock, and it will be opened to you. For everyone who asks receives, and the one who seeks finds, and to the one who knocks it will be opened. Or which one of you, if his son asks him for bread, will give him a stone? Or if he asks for a fish, will give him a serpent? If you then, who are evil, know how to give good gifts to your children, how much more will your Father who is in heaven give good things to those who ask him! Matthew 7:7-11*

Note that Jesus Christ didn't call the Pharisees wicked just because they killed somebody but because they had lived a life of lies which was equivalent to evil in the sight of God. Any unrighteous man that lives has a bed of roses that is full of wickedness and every of his actions are ordained by that very thought of him.

Wickedness comes from sin, sin comes from Satan and all have judgments placed upon them by God unto destruction. *But now that you have been set free from sin and have become slaves of God, the fruit you get leads to sanctification and its end, eternal life. For the wages of sin is death, but the free gift of God is eternal life in Christ Jesus our Lord. Romans 6:22-23*

Because of the grave sin the Lord has ordained it to be, the heart of wickedness is subject to death by God. Every form of unholy thoughts will be Judged, been matched into ashes by the holy act of God.

Although what Christ has done has brought liberation unto all men and he has set them free from every work of the wicked, howbeit, some believers still exhibit this act of wickedness. Firstly, it is our wickedness that makes a man not to love God.

Because of the disposition of the mind, so many Christians are so content eating the bit of the word. Not willing to expound more into more truth. Many claim they live for Christ but never willing to fellowship with the brethren, study the word, pray or even fellowship with the spirit. God has ordained that every man will live in a certain way. *This Book of the Law shall not depart from your mouth, but you shall meditate on it day and night, so that you may be careful to do according to all that is written in it. For then you will make your way prosperous, and then you will have good success. Joshua 1:8*
Praying at all times in the Spirit, with all prayer and supplication. To that end, keep alert with all perseverance, making supplication for all the saints Ephesians 6:18

These activities of meditating on the word and consistent lifestyle of prayer are important for a true life of fellowship with the light. These activities change the wickedness of the human mind to see the glory of God through His son and to become the righteousness of God at heart.

The mindset of the Lord is to have people rigorous from his work and do everything possible to please him. Every virtue of the devil is wickedness, therefore to get man; he just implants the seed of wickedness into their heart.

When the seed of wickedness is imputed into a man's heart, every of his actions will be wicked in the sight of God.

Also, wickedness is a form of life. God's light has been made available for all to enjoy and eat from as much as we can contain. It is quite surprising that men will choose darkness over light all because of their wicked nature. *And this is the judgment: the light has come into the world, and people loved the darkness rather than the light because their works were evil. John 3:19*

Most of the ways of many Christians nowadays are full of unrighteous act, even though they know about the ways of God. Many dwell in that form of darkness knowing the light of God. Paul made a strong warning to believers in the scripture, understanding the cunning ways to the devil to impart his kind of life unto humanity.

Wickedness is an act that God condemns, every Christian is to flee from this acts and life, and embrace the fellowship of the Lord which light unto our soul.

PRAYER POINT: *Lord Jesus, I am sorry for my wicked and evil acts. I bow at your feet and ask for forgiveness. Cleanse me oh God and make me a new creature.*

MATERIALISM

But people who long to be rich fall into temptation and are trapped by many foolish and harmful desires that plunge them into ruin and destruction. For the love of money is the root of all kinds of evil. And some people, craving money, have wandered from the true faith and pierced themselves with many sorrows. 1 Timothy 6:9-10

MATERIALISM

But people who long to be rich fall into temptation and are trapped by many foolish and harmful desires that plunge them into ruin and destruction. For the love of money is the root of all kinds of evil. And some people, craving money, have wandered from the true faith and pierced themselves with many sorrows. 1 Timothy 6:9-10

Materialism is usually associated with physical things. An individual that is said to be materialistic usually is a lover of the physical things. Materialism is always a form of life that is preoccupied with material things rather than the knowledge to be gained.

Christians are not only necessarily the only culprit in the case as God has come to save every man. The work of God is for all and sundry. And one of the things he did through his salvation is to bless us with everything we would need. *Blessed be the God and Father of our Lord Jesus Christ, who has blessed us in Christ with every spiritual blessing in the heavenly places, 4 even as he chose us in him before the foundation of the world, that we should be holy and blameless before him in love. Ephesians 1:3-4*

These opportunities in Christ has been made available for all and as many that are ready to accept Christ, accept him and continue in his ways as he given the chance to enjoy every of these benefits. Therefore, every human being is naturally destined to live not according to the love of this world but the blessing from God and his son through his spirit.

The sight and likeness for the things that are seen are usually dangerous; firstly, the things that are seen are carnal. The word carnal does not necessarily means sinful, but usually it refers to an entity that can perish and is subject to corruption. One thing we must understand about all these physical things is that they will pass away, washed by the power of God upon the earth. *Heaven and earth will pass away, but my words will not pass away. Mat 24:35*

Everything that we can see, love physically, admire physical are all subject to corruption for they shall wither and become dust. Even the human body grows old every day because one day, it will pass away. Therefore, it is important that the sight of men should translate beyond the physical things that are seen but unto a more glorious ending of eternal matters.

Another thing that is usually that comes to mind is a level of Ignorance. Ignorance is not necessarily, not knowing sometimes, but inability to activate that knowledge. If believers understand the things that God has put in store for them, they will be dismay but the abundance of riches that has been kept for them ready to be unveiled in a pure way.

Every needs and desires of the child of God has been known even from ages past by the Lord and he has made proper provision for all these things. Now take this clue, everything that God made, he made provision for their sustenance, not just to have but to have in abundance. Every believer has been ordained unto a life of riches and enjoyment because of the provision of Christ. *If you then, who are evil, know how to give good gifts to your children, how much more will your Father who is in heaven give good things to those who ask him! Mat 7:11*

Because of these provisions that he has made, we are not born to strive and this is the strength we have in Christ Jesus. It is the wickedness and greediness of the heart that makes believers and cohorts become materialists, fixing their gaze upon the physical things rather than the thing of God.

Because of the desires of mankind, the wishes that has accumulated over time, many fall into this trap and love physical material so much that they fail to recognize their falling. This is not to say that Christians are not to be rich or have enough, like it has been said, every Christian is ordained unto great life and prosperity. *And if you are Christ's, then you are Abraham's offspring, heirs according to promise. Galatians 3:29*

Anything that takes the place of God in our heart is sin and subject to destruction. Our whole lives should be placed on him and we must continually behold God. Any form of fascination, obsession or preoccupation with a thing outside God is evil in the sight of God. Every of our souls, strength should be dedicated to God and his works. *Hear, O Israel: The Lord our God, the Lord is one. You shall love the Lord your God with all your heart and with all your soul and with all your might. And these words that I command you today shall be on your heart. Deuteronomy 6:4-6*

Anything that is physical cannot bring the true riches that we care for (Pro 10:22). It is only God that can bring true riches our way without the fear of perishing. That is why he has given us a commandment to look away from all these physical things, and bestow our gaze upon him, looking at his son and the works. Seeking his things and the success, progression, establishment of his life.

The kingdom of God doesn't contain in the things that are seen, the command is keep doing his will, obey his voice always, keep to his word and every other thing, including the money, the houses, every satisfaction that we crave for will be given to us without stress and in peace.

Therefore we must stop every form of human cunning attitudes to get rich, swaying people back and forth because of the love for physical things, we must engage in the things of the Lord and his word, daily equipping ourselves with instruments to make his kingdom work and his life progress among the gentiles. These are the ways of his kingdom which is the prerequisite to my real success. *The end of the matter; all has been heard. Fear God and keep his commandments, for this is the whole duty of man. Ecclesiastes 12:13*

PRAYER POINT: *Lord Jesus, please turn my heart toward your statutes and not toward selfish gain. Turn my eyes away from worthless things; preserve my life according to your word.*

DOCTRINES

Do not be carried away by all kinds of strange teachings.
(Hebrews 13:9)
"Beware of the false prophets, who come to you in sheep's clothing, but
inwardly are ravenous wolves." (Matt. 7:15)

DOCTRINES

Religion and the act of been pious is a disease that has eaten deep into many Christians. While it is great to have a people that are always diligent about ensuring the physical things of God move rightly, it is important that we don't get too religious about these things as it may hinder the quality of our service to God.

Religion is the act of piety, ability to be physically diligent in the things of God. Note that these are all physically activities that cannot give us spiritual blessings

The practice of religion is an act of ignorance displayed by Christians, where emphasis is more on works than faith and fellowship with God. It is always a cunning safe house to be, as many who do that tries to hide under the shadow of religion and think is service to God.

It is so sad that the church has been turned to a religious gathering based on the carnal nature of men. Let's understand that the things of God cannot be physically done without the Spirit of God it is impossible for us to have the Spirit of God, follow His ways and being religion blinded.

Religion blindfolds the heart of the believer to make physical sacrifices unto God. While it is a great thing to be religious because been religious means piety, the act of been physical diligent with the things of God. Going regularly to church, reading your bible consistently, listening to messages consistently are all paths of religion and sometimes a Christian can get so blinded by those physical activities and aren't deeply into God's will and desire.

Paul spoke about how people will come to be blinded, prophesying about the things that are to be and what they might entail. *Do not be carried away by all kinds of strange teachings. (Hebrews 13:9)*

We must be careful so that we don't get caught up in the things that men will praise us for than the things of the spirit. It is impossible to please God by being religious but by our walk of defining truth and purity unto God. When a church celebrates the outward appearance of the things of God than the Spiritual life, it is impossible for the church not to enter a dangerous zone and begin to worship mammon.

Religion is an act that has eaten deep into the church, having gatherings that basically do rehearsals of the things that are shown and never given chances to the things of the spirit; we must be careful so that we don't slip away into the act of religion that will take us from what the spirit has to communicate to us.

When we let so much of our activities revolve a physical rehearsal and forget what the spirit wants, it is impossible not to be a slave to religion.

Those that are blinded by religion are usually headed for destruction. The Devil uses that as an avenue to gain access to their service unto God and corrupt their minds He takes a hold of their minds, and makes it resistant to the truth of God's word.

When a man tries so much to assist the spirit with a lot of physical methods and ways, the man becomes addicted to religion, never open to learning but taken away by that blindfold that shields away from the light. The light of God's word is usually not able to easily penetrate their hearts because of the blindfold. *And even if our gospel is veiled, it is veiled to those who are perishing. In their case the god of this world has blinded the minds of the unbelievers, to keep them from seeing the light of the gospel of the glory of Christ, who is the image of God. 2Corinthians 4:3-4*

Because of the religion they so much cherish, the people will not be able to receive God's light. Religion causes problem by shielding them away from the truth causing them to be people of zeal and strength without the power of God.

What the blindfold of religion brings is loads of doctrines, bringing to naught sound doctrines among the brethren and giving them worldly doctrines that are not of God. *I appeal to you, brothers, to watch out for those who cause divisions and create obstacles contrary to the doctrine that you have been taught; avoid them. Romans 16:17*

Doctrine is defined by the word **teaching**. Doctrine is an outflow of what is in stock; and that is why corruption of the body by religion will cause false doctrines to be taught among men. We must understand that doctrine is one of the pillars that make up a Christian's faith and life, a detriment in doctrine may lead to so many fallible exercises. Men taking away from the way of God, and led by their minds and worldly concepts that they have been taught, a moment of mistake in sound doctrine may lead to so many troubles for a believer, for the local assembly and for the church community at large. One of the forces of false doctrine is the heart; every move that is made in the heart and captured by the heart is usually the main source of an individual mentality.

False doctrine takes up the nature of the heart and forms thoughts, mindset, will, emotion and form the way of life for a man. *For such persons do not serve our Lord Christ, but their own appetites, and by smooth talk and flattery they deceive the hearts of the naive. Romans 16:18*

Once the heart is taken by this doctrine, it is usually impossible to change a man from his stand and such a man only need the mercy of God to save him from wrath. We must all rise up as believers so that we can keep the true doctrine, void of very excessive religious mentality and full of the way of the life of God as an instruction of God to his people. *"Go and stand in the temple and speak to the people all the words of this Life." Act 5:20*

The essence of these instructions is to ensure we stay on our guard so that we are not taken away by false doctrines. One of the things that God wants for his children is the ability to grow up and form a mindset that cannot be shaken. If a Christian understands the life of God in him, he will not be swayed by every wind of doctrine that comes around. Rooted and grounded in the words of the apostles. To equip the saints for the work of ministry, for building up the body of Christ, until we all attain to the unity of the faith and of the knowledge of the Son of God, to mature manhood, to the measure of the stature of the fullness of Christ, so that we may no longer be children, tossed to and fro by the waves and carried about by every wind of doctrine, by human cunning, by craftiness in deceitful schemes. Ephesians 4:12-14

Every form of false doctrine will bring about destruction. There will always be a destruction that awaits those that fall into the act of false doctrine. God's wrath and judgment will come upon those that fall into this act. *So in the present case I tell you, keep away from these men and let them alone, for if this plan or this undertaking is of man, it will fail. Act 5:38*

Every ordination and doctrine of men will always fail and they will be destroyed at the end of the day. Though it may seem to have its own successes, it will surely fail at the end and bring forth wastage unto the people that are within its frame.

It is essential that amongst us, we clear every form of religious mindset, religious acts, religious dealings, religious doings and religious teaching so that we don't fall prey to false doctrines and lead the people of God unto destruction.

PRAYER POINT: *Dear Lord, please deliver me from the hackles of religion and make me obey your word daily.*

PRIDE

By the mouth of a fool comes a rod for his back, but the lips of the wise will preserve them   Proverb 14:3

PRIDE

We sometimes think of ourselves as being better or more righteous than the next man. We look for areas in our lives to pin-point as areas that we haven't failed at. However, we fail to remember that those habits are usually set up by activities around that try to beguile us. Men have a usual habit of tentatively been gentle in the act of no serious or major events that can uproot every form of bad habits that is in that man.

One thing that must be understood is that pride is an act of the inability of man to listen to the humility that God gives. When a man is full of himself and cannot be brought down by the word God, he will always be pompous and full of pride.

There are so many causes of pride; these causes are usually not the source but the cause of it. Every man has an element of pride in him except he is worked upon by the spirit of God, when a man is not worked upon and these causes come, they bring out the nature of that man. And shows him who he is and what he comprises inside.

The first thing that can cause pride is **knowledge**. We must understand that knowledge in its own is not bad as knowledge is essential for growth, but knowledge that is not guided will always lead to pomposity. *(1 Corinthians 8:1-2)*

Knowledge that is not well informed will always lead to pride. Every form of knowing must be guided by patience, wisdom and long suffering so that they can be perfect, wanting nothing.

Another cause of pride is the **fullness of riches**, men glory a lot in their physical wealth and abilities, forgetting the things that God has done for them. *(Luke 12:16-20)*

When a man so much glory in the things that he has, the riches, the wealth, the physical abilities and all, failing to acknowledge God in the process, such person will always be proud.

Sometimes, many don't know they have fallen prey to this. Men unconsciously become proud in their hearts and they might not know it. Going about, bouncing in the wealth of what they physically have. Some people take pride in the awards they have, some pastor's pride in the miracles they have done in the past and claim a right to respect because of that, losing hold of the humility they are supposed to have and losing hold of what they are supposed to be in Christ.

The end of pride is always destruction, since God has hates pride; he limits a lot of blessing from them. *Pride goes before destruction and a haughty spirit before a fall. Proverbs 16:18*
But he gives more grace. Therefore, it says, "God opposes the proud but gives grace to the humble." James 4:6

Many things that the Lord gives people always exude proud. Many will fall short of God's blessings because of the state of their heart towards God. Because the proud cannot manage God's property as he wants, God cannot bless him. *The reason is because the standards of God are usually based on humility, every man that wants to learn God must be subjected to humility. (Phil 2:3-8)*

God only lifts up the humble, God does not dwell in the realm of pride and he doesn't hail those that dwell in it. Therefore, as Christians, we must learn from God, believing His every word and making it effectual in our lives so that we may eat of the fruit of the land.

PRAYER POINT: *Lord, teach me your ways and let me learn your humility, so that I can become like you.*

REGAINING

SIGHT

The steadfast love of the Lord never ceases; his mercies never come to an end; they are new every morning, great is your faithfulness
Lamentation 3:22-23

REGAINING SIGHT

E ven though God is a consuming fire and doesn't take anything for granted in the life of His people, He still always has plans for the default-ers. The fact that men may have failed one way or the other is not enough for God to discard them, for as many that comes back to Him, He always receives them, forgive them and deal with them as one that has never sinned. Giving them everything they should have enjoyed.

The parable of the prodigal son was taught by Christ. There was a son who asked for his belongings from his father while he was still alive, he got the resources and walked to a far land. While in the far land, he wasted all his resources, spending it on frivolities and wasting it on things that can never last.

After all his suffering, he came back to his father, falling down at his feet, with the hope that his father will make him just a servant but the father made him a son. In his explanation, Jesus related the son to believers that have strayed away and they have now come back. *Just so, I tell you, there will be more joy in heaven over one sinner who repents than over ninety-nine righteous persons who need no repentance. Luke 15:7*

God dwells in so much Joy when any of His son that has strayed away comes back. He lavishes upon them as He should have by granting them enough access into the things that He has and brings them to the position He wants them to be.

In getting back the light that has been lost, the first thing a person must understand is how to receive the life of God again. *In him was life, and the life was the light of men. The light shines in the darkness, and the darkness has not overcome it. John 1:4-5*

Because of the content of the life of God, the life is the light for every man. In getting back sight, a man must identify his bad ways, repent and receive the life of God in his soul. The life of God will cause light to shine upon him and he will be able to see. The source of this life is the word of God; a Christian must ensure that he is rooted in the word of God, ensuring total obedience to the commandments of God from His words. *The unfolding of your words gives light; it imparts understanding to the simple. Psalm 119:130*

When a man is opened to God in his heart and he receives life, there will be an influx of light and men will see. They will walk in the right path, getting the fullness of the truth God wants to communicate.

PRAYER POINT: *Lord, I receive your light; please help me to walk rightly in your ways.*

ABOUT THE AUTHOR

Damilola Gbadamosi is a graduate of Towson University with a bachelor's degree in business administration and Electronic business. She is currently a graduate student at University of Maryland studying cyber security. She loves arts including painting, poetry, and literature. She is a writer, singer, presenter, and an actress. She has written a couple of poems and hopes to publish an anthology of poems someday. As a believer and follower of Jesus Christ she has a passion to reach and encourage the younger generation to find their purpose in life. She has a passion for the homeless and volunteers whenever she can. Damilola is an advocate against abuse most especially emotional abuse. She is the founder of Gods Generation which is a generation of youths on fire for God.

www.ingramcontent.com/pod-product-compliance
Lightning Source LLC
Chambersburg PA
CBHW060141050426
42448CB00010B/2243